ISAAC ASIMOV'S NEW LIBRARY OF THE UNIVERSE

ASTRONOMY PROJECTS

BY ISAAC ASIMOV
WITH REVISIONS AND UPDATING BY GREG WALZ-CHOJNACKI

Gareth Stevens Publishing
MILWAUKEE

For a free color catalog describing Gareth Stevens' list of high-quality books, call 1-800-542-2595 (USA) or 1-800-461-9120 (Canada). Gareth Stevens' Fax: (414) 225-0377.

Library of Congress Cataloging-in-Publication Data

Asimov, Isaac.
  Astronomy projects / by Isaac Asimov; with revisions and updating
by Greg Walz-Chojnacki.
    p. cm. — (Isaac Asimov's New library of the universe)
  Rev. ed. of: Projects in astronomy. 1990.
  Includes index.
  Summary: Presents a variety of astronomy projects, including
creative writing and drawing assignments, modelmaking, sky
observation, and experiments.
  ISBN 0-8368-1229-8
  1. Astronomy—Study and teaching—Activity programs—Juvenile
literature. [1. Astronomy projects. 2. Astronomy. 3. Science projects.]
I. Walz-Chojnacki, Greg, 1954-. II. Asimov, Isaac. Projects in astronomy.
III. Title. IV. Series: Asimov, Isaac. New library of the universe.
QB64.A75 1996
520'.78—dc20   95-40379

This edition first published in 1996 by
Gareth Stevens Publishing
1555 North RiverCenter Drive, Suite 201
Milwaukee, Wisconsin 53212, USA

Project editor: Barbara J. Behm
Design adaptation: Helene Feider
Editorial assistant: Diane Laska
Production director: Teresa Mahsem
Picture research: Matthew Groshek and Diane Laska
Illustrations: Tom Redman

Printed in the United States of America

1 2 3 4 5 6 7 8 9 99 98 97 96

To bring this classic of young people's information up to date, the editors at Gareth Stevens Publishing have selected two noted science authors, Greg Walz-Chojnacki and Francis Reddy. Walz-Chojnacki and Reddy coauthored the recent book *Celestial Delights: The Best Astronomical Events Through 2001.*

Walz-Chojnacki is also the author of the book *Comet: The Story Behind Halley's Comet* and various articles about the space program. He was an editor of *Odyssey*, an astronomy and space technology magazine for young people, for eleven years.

Reddy is the author of nine books, including *Halley's Comet, Children's Atlas of the Universe, Children's Atlas of Earth Through Time*, and *Children's Atlas of Native Americans*, plus numerous articles. He was an editor of *Astronomy* magazine for several years.

CONTENTS

We live in an enormously large place – the Universe. It's just in the last fifty-five years or so that we've found out how large it probably is. It's only natural that we would want to understand the place in which we live, so scientists have developed instruments – such as radio telescopes, satellites, probes, and many more – that have told us far more about the Universe than could possibly be imagined.

We have seen planets up close. We have learned about quasars and pulsars, black holes, and supernovas. We have gathered amazing data about how the Universe may have come into being and how it may end. Nothing could be more astonishing.

Every day, astronomers and other scientists work to further understand the Universe. Reading about their discoveries is exciting, but doing your own science projects is the best way to truly discover the mysteries of the Universe. With the projects in this book, you will make craters, build a constellation clock and the Solar System in a shoebox, and much more. It's your turn to be a scientist!

Isaac Asimov

Project 1:
A Cosmic Dance –
Earth and the Moon

Earth and the Moon have been in a cosmic dance for billions of years. The Moon appears to change its shape as it orbits Earth each month. It sometimes appears as a slim crescent. At other times, it looks like a bright white disk. These changes, called the Moon's phases, occur because every night a slightly different fraction of the Moon's sunlit side is revealed to us as the Moon orbits Earth.

Studying an Earth-Moon model makes the Moon's phases much easier to understand. But don't forget to observe the real thing!

Purpose of the project:
To observe that the phases of the Moon are the result of the relationship between Earth, the Moon, and the Sun.

What you'll need:
• String
• A bright light, such as a bulb without a shade
• A ball, such as a soccer ball

What to do:
To learn about the Moon's phases, create a model of the Sun, Moon, and Earth. First, with some string, outline a circle on the floor underneath a strong light source. Stand or sit in the middle of the circle. The light represents the Sun, you represent Earth, and the circle represents the Moon's path around Earth. Have a friend hold a ball – the "Moon" – so the light shines on it. While your friend walks around the circle, watch the changing shape of the lighted portion of the ball.

Repeat the experiment, this time letting your friend stand or sit while you act out the part of the "Moon." This experiment will work only if you have a single light source in an otherwise darkened room or area.

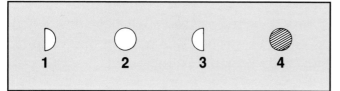

Above: The shape of the Moon appears to change as it orbits Earth. These changes are called phases. During the different phases, we see a slightly different fraction of the Moon's sunlit side in the night sky over a month's time.

Key to the Moon's phases as viewed from Earth:
(1) first quarter　　(3) last quarter
(2) full Moon　　　　(4) new Moon

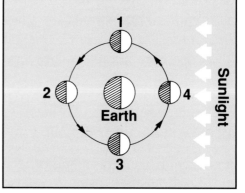

Above: A diagram representing the Earth-Moon system shows that the side of the Moon facing the Sun is always illuminated.

Project 2:
Was There Water on Mars?

The planet Mars is drier than the driest desert on Earth. Water would simply boil away in its thin atmosphere. But, as scientists learned in the 1970s, Mars was not always this way. Space probes have revealed dried-up river channels on the Red Planet's surface.

The channels were probably carved by brief, muddy floods, not by the types of rivers that are found on Earth. Ice beneath Mars's soil probably melted, creating a flow of mud and rock that etched the channels. By building a simple model of the Martian surface, you can study how the planet might be affected by flowing water.

Below: This photograph, taken by a probe, shows a series of dried-up channels on Mars. The channels were probably caused by muddy floods long ago.

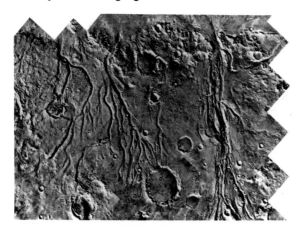

Purpose of the project:
To recreate the effects of erosion in order to understand how Mars's surface became the way it is today.

What you'll need:
- A waterproof box – this can be anything from a baking pan to a wooden box lined with plastic. The experiment works best with a wide, shallow box.
- Water, and something to pour it from – either a garden hose or a large pitcher
- Several bricks or wooden blocks
- Sand and various other materials, such as gravel, top soil, flour, and small rocks

What to do:
Fill the box with sand. Be sure to pack it firmly. Set the box up at an angle, as shown in the picture, using bricks or wooden blocks to hold it in position.

Pour water from the hose or pitcher onto the sand at the top of the box, gradually at first, then a greater amount. Watch how the water cuts channels in the sand as the water flows down the box.

When you have made a number of "valleys," compare your landscape with this photograph of Mars. Do they look similar?

What happens if you freeze the box of "valleys?" Can you simulate a "Mars-quake" by flexing the frozen material to crack the soil?

Clean out the box and try the experiment again. This time, after you put sand in the box, add some small rocks. Watch how the rocks divert the flow of water.

You might also try packing the sand loosely and watching how this speeds erosion. Finally, pack the box with alternating layers of sand, gravel, top soil, and flour. The resulting Martian "canyons" should show different layers, or strata, just like natural canyons on Earth!

Project 3:
Impact Craters

The planets were formed when chunks of debris in space clumped together to form larger and larger planet-size chunks. Some of the smaller debris still floats through the Solar System. When this debris strikes a planet or moon, the impact gouges out a huge hole, or crater, in the surface of the planet or moon.

There are only about a hundred known impact craters to be found on Earth today. Wind and rain have worn away all but the largest. But there are thousands on Mercury, Mars, Earth's Moon, and the many other moons in the Solar System. In this project, you'll study how craters form.

Below: Impact craters give Earth's Moon its special appearance. This close-up shows the variety of sizes and styles of lunar craters.

Purpose of the project:
To show how craters are formed and to understand the different shapes they take.

What you'll need:
- A waterproof box, just like the one used in Project 2
- Top soil and flour
- Water and a sprinkling can
- Several marbles or pebbles
- A chair or stepladder

What to do:
Place a waterproof box flat on the ground and fill it with top soil. Sprinkle water over the top soil until it has a muddy consistency. Place a chair or stepladder next to the box and carefully climb up on it.

Drop a few marbles or pebbles one by one into the mud. What kinds of "craters" do they make? Try throwing some marbles into the mud from different angles. Throw some pebbles very hard, then lightly. Compare your results with the picture of the Moon on this page. Do the lunar craters look similar to yours?

To create a different effect, clean out the box and redo the experiment. This time, add more water to make the mud much softer. Throw the marbles or pebbles in. Notice how the runnier mud beneath fills up all but the largest craters, just like the "seas" on the Moon.

Set up the experiment again, without any water this time. Fill the box with layers of differently colored "soils" (for example, flour and top soil). When you drop the marbles or pebbles, notice how the craters reveal the layer underneath and how some of the "soil" splashes onto the surface.

Project 4:
One Size and Distance Does Not Fit All

Our Solar System consists of the Sun, nine known planets (including Earth), dozens of moons, thousands of asteroids, and perhaps billions of distant comets.

The innermost planets to the Sun – Mercury, Venus, Earth, and Mars – are made mostly of iron and rock. The outer planets – Jupiter, Saturn, Uranus, and Neptune – are huge balls of gas. Far-flung Pluto is an oddity, a tiny frozen gas ball.

You'll need plenty of space for this project, which will help you appreciate just how big our Solar System is.

Purpose of the project:
To understand the incredible size of our Solar System by making a model of the distance between the Sun and Earth to scale.

What you'll need:
- A large beach ball
- A tape measure
- A pea
- A large open area, such as a soccer field

What to do:
Most models of our Solar System make the planets seem far bigger and closer together than they really are. To understand the actual sizes and distances, give a friend a beach ball and have her or him stand at one end of an athletic field, such as a soccer field. Put the pea in your hand, and walk 200 feet (61 meters) away from your friend toward the other end of the field. Turn around and look back. If the Sun were the size of your friend's beach ball, Earth would be the size of the pea. The distance between the two of you is how far apart the Earth and Sun would be.

It would take many friends and a very big field to make a complete model of our Solar System. For instance, the planet Mercury would be a tiny grain of sand in your hand about 80 feet (24 m) from the beach-ball Sun. That's nearly the distance from base to base on a baseball diamond. Grapefruit-size Jupiter would be over 1,000 feet (305 m) from the "Sun." That's the distance of over three soccer fields laid end to end. And Pluto, the tiniest and most distant planet, would also be a grain of sand, 1.5 miles (2.4 kilometers) from the "Sun!" If you can find a big enough area, you could get together with some friends and play the roles of some of the planets. Line up the appropriate distances away from the beach-ball Sun and start walking around the Sun in your "orbits." Everyone should be sure to walk at the same pace. Who finishes first? Check other books in Isaac Asimov's *New Library of the Universe* to see how your results compare with the time it takes each of the actual planets to make an orbit of the Sun.

Project 5:
Solar System in a Shoebox

The range in size between the largest and smallest bodies in our Solar System is huge. You could fit over 920 Jupiters inside the Sun and 270,000 Plutos inside Jupiter.

Interestingly, the four largest planets – Jupiter, Saturn, Uranus, and Neptune – all have rocky centers about the size of Earth and Venus. They are larger because of the vast amount of gas each of them collected when they formed. Jupiter, Saturn, Uranus, and Neptune each have enough hydrogen to equal the mass of several Earths.

This project is an exciting way to keep a miniature Solar System in your room. Although the relative sizes of the planets are approximate and the distances between them won't be to scale, you'll be able to appreciate the sizes of the Sun and planets in a shoebox!

Purpose of the project:
To appreciate the enormous differences between the sizes of the bodies in our Solar System.

What you'll need:
- A shoebox
- Markers or colored pencils
- Posterboard
- Black paint
- Glue
- Tape
- Twist ties
- Scissors

What to do:
Photocopy the shapes on the opposite page. Glue the photocopy to posterboard. Color the shapes to match the features of each planet. (You can find this information from other books in *Isaac Asimov's New Library of the Universe* series.) Cut out each shape with scissors.

Paint the inside of a shoebox black. When the paint is dry, make slits in the bottom of the box where you want to position your planets. Gently glue the planets onto the ends of twist ties. Slide the free ends of the twist ties through the slits. Bend down the ends, and tape them to the outside of the box.

Below: An example of what your Solar System in a shoebox might look like.

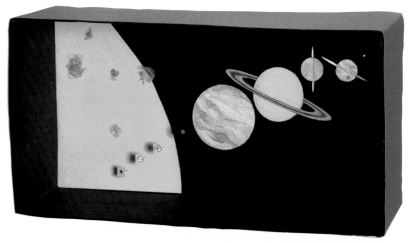

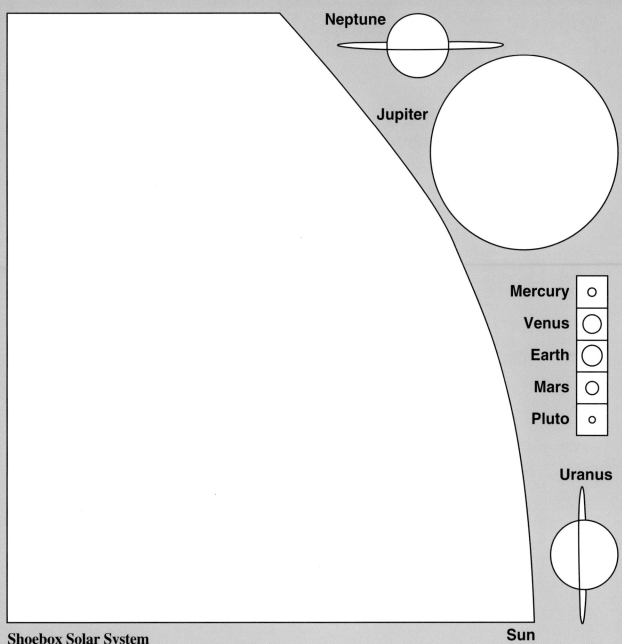

Neptune

Jupiter

Mercury	○
Venus	○
Earth	○
Mars	○
Pluto	○

Uranus

Sun

Shoebox Solar System

Sun and Planets	Actual Diameters	Planets	Actual Diameters
Sun	865,000 miles (1,391,785 km)	Jupiter	88,720 miles (142,775 km)
Mercury	3,031 miles (4,877 km)	Saturn	74,557 miles (119,983 km)
Venus	7,519 miles (12,100 km)	Uranus	31,494 miles (50,683 km)
Earth	7,926 miles (12,755 km)	Neptune	29,995 miles (48,270 km)
Mars	4,334 miles (6,975 km)	Pluto	1,429 miles (2,300 km)

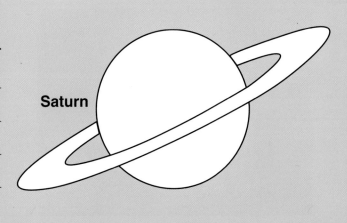

Saturn

Project 6:
Colors of the Rainbow – the Spectrum

Light from the Sun looks white, but it actually is a combination of many colors. These colors reveal themselves only when sunlight passes through a substance that causes the light to bend. The result is a rainbow pattern of color – red to orange, yellow to green, blue to violet. This display of colors is called a spectrum.

Light is the visible portion of the larger electromagnetic spectrum, which includes X rays, ultraviolet radiation, heat, and radio waves. Keep this in mind as you make your own spectrum in this project.

Below: A rainbow is a spectrum caused by sunlight passing through droplets of water in the air. This double rainbow occurred over the Badlands in South Dakota.

Purpose of the project:
To refract, or bend, light, showing how sunlight is actually made up of many different colors.

What you'll need:
- A garden hose
- A shallow bowl
- Water
- A small mirror
- Sunlight
- A white wall or white posterboard
- A small stone or lump of clay

What to do:
A rainbow is a naturally occurring spectrum. Rainbows are caused by sunlight passing through drops of rain in the air. The moisture acts like a prism and breaks up the sunlight into the colors of the spectrum. You can make your own miniature rainbow with a garden hose on a sunny day. Turn on the water and partially cover the end of the hose with your thumb to create a fine mist. Stand so that the Sun is directly behind you, and aim the water away from the Sun. With just a little adjustment, you should be able to spot a spectrum shimmering in the spray of water. It is your own private rainbow!

Inset: In this experiment, you will create a spectrum out of sunlight. The diagram shows how to arrange the different items in this project. First, fill a shallow bowl with clean water. Place the bowl in direct sunlight. Put a small mirror in the bowl, using a small stone or lump of clay to hold the mirror upright. Arrange the mirror so it reflects the light onto the wall. If a white wall is not available, tape a piece of white posterboard to the wall where the reflected light falls.

In combination with the mirror, the water should act as a prism to break up the white sunlight and project a many-colored spectrum. What colors do you see on the wall? In what order?

sunlight

mirror

water

spectrum

stone

Project 7:
It's Raining Meteors!

Some night when you're out under a clear, dark sky, you may be surprised to see one or more bright streaks across the sky. Most will disappear so fast they will be gone before you can tell anyone else to look. But a few will last several seconds, lighting up that area of the sky and trailing smoke. These are meteors, flaming encounters between small, fast-moving space debris and Earth's atmosphere.

Several times a year, Earth runs through the extra-dusty orbit of a comet. This creates a meteor shower, and your chance of seeing meteors increases greatly!

Below: A blazing meteor is caught by the camera as it flashes through the starry sky.

Project 8:
Binoculars Bring the Universe Closer

Binoculars can reveal some delightful astronomical sights. They show a larger piece of the sky than a telescope does, and they can be carried along on any trip.

What can you see in the sky with binoculars? An up-close view of the Moon's cratered face or the four largest moons of Jupiter are easy to spot. With binoculars, you can see bright star clusters with their dense fields of stars. What looks like fuzzy greenish stars are gas clouds called nebulae!

Opposite: Two views of the star cluster Pleiades – one as seen with the unaided eye *(left)*, the other as viewed through a pair of binoculars *(right)*. This star cluster is also known as the Seven Sisters. The binoculars reveal more and also fainter stars than the naked eye, including the seventh "sister."

Purpose of the project:
To observe and discover the Universe with binoculars.

What you'll need:
- A good pair of binoculars
- A clear night
- A dark place from where you can observe the sky
- An almanac or newspaper and a star map

What to do:
When using binoculars, be sure to sit or stand in a comfortable position. If you can, rest your elbows or lean against a fence or tree to steady yourself.

Look at the Moon and compare what you see against the drawings from Project 1. What features of the Moon do you observe? Use an almanac or newspaper to find out which planets are currently visible, or if there are any upcoming eclipses of the Moon. Can you see Jupiter's moons or the phases of Venus?

Try to find certain stars, galaxies, and nebulae. Locate the Pleiades (the Seven Sisters) or any other star cluster. Then compare what you see with and without binoculars. Do the same with the three stars that make up Orion's sword. One of them is a star-birthing nebula – can you tell which? Use a star map to find other nebulae.

See if you can tell which star in the Big Dipper is really a double star. Are there any other double stars? Look at the Milky Way. What features can only be seen using binoculars? Can you find any of the Milky Way's dark nebulae?

Finally, try to locate the Andromeda Galaxy, the farthest object in the sky that can be seen without a telescope. To the unaided eye, it's just a dim, misty spot in the darkness. But with binoculars and a bit of luck, you can see it more clearly – from where you are on Earth, 2.3 million light-years away!

Project 9:
Build Your Own Planetarium

City lights dim our view of the stars. For many people, a visit to a planetarium is the only way to see a bright, starry sky. A planetarium projects light through thousands of tiny holes onto a domed ceiling. Each hole represents a star in a constellation. A planetarium can recreate a starry sky as seen from any place on Earth – and for any night during the next 26,000 years!

You can construct your own planetarium from materials around the house!

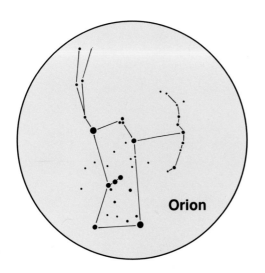
Orion

Purpose of the project:
To design and build a home planetarium

What you'll need:
- A flashlight
- Dark cardboard
- Scissors
- Tape
- A pushpin
- A pencil
- A star map
- Black paper or black paint
- A cardboard tube, slightly bigger around than the flashlight

What to do:
Unscrew and remove the lens from a flashlight *(figure 1, next page)*. Cover it with black paper and then place it back on the flashlight *(figure 2)*.

Paint the inside of a cardboard tube black or line it with black paper. Cut out a piece of dark cardboard and fit it onto one end of the cardboard tube. Cut a hole in this cardboard so that the tube fits around the flashlight. Place the tube around the flashlight, and tape over any cracks that would let light through. This is your projector *(figure 3)*.

Cut several disks out of dark cardboard, each large enough to completely cover the open end of the tube. With a pencil, draw constellations on them from your star map, or photocopy the disks on these pages and use them as models. Using a pushpin, carefully make a hole where each star should be. For the brighter stars, make larger holes. Tape a disk into place over the flashlight, making sure no light gets out except through the star holes. When you place the disk into the projector, be sure that the star patterns are not projecting backward.

Now you're ready to try out your projector. In a darkened room, shine the flashlight onto a wall. You will observe star patterns just as they appear in the sky. Your projector will help you spot the actual night-sky constellations by making you more familiar with them.

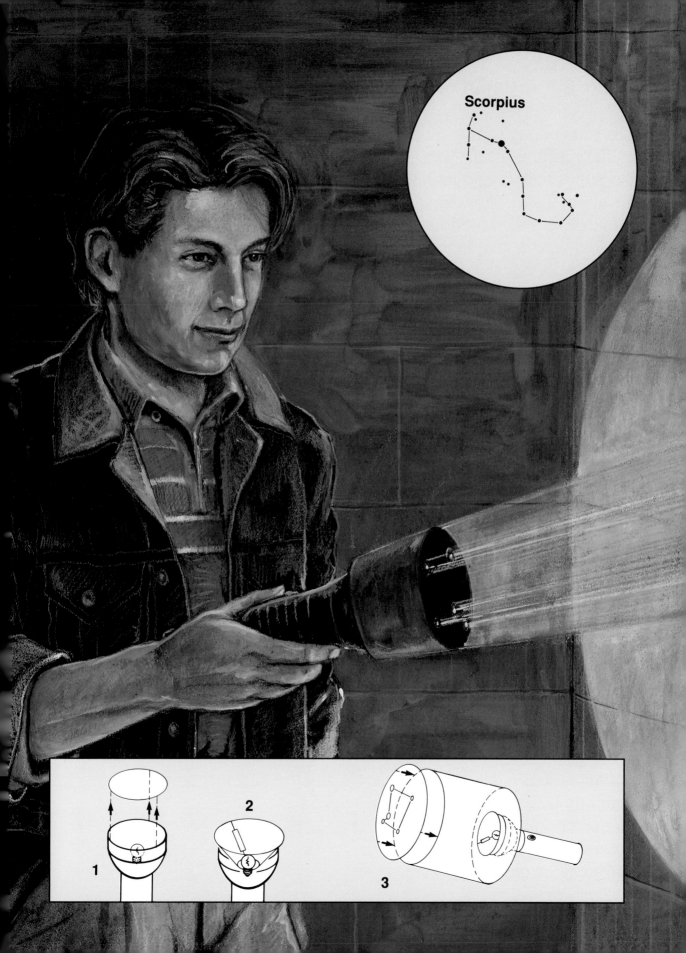

Scorpius

Project 10:
Make a Constellation Clock

The time of day can be estimated by the positions of the Sun. When the Sun is halfway up in the sky, it's about 9 a.m. At noon, the Sun is on the so-called meridian. The meridian is the imaginary line between north and south in the sky.

At night, the stars can be used to tell time. But stars do not take the same position at midnight every night of the year, as the Sun does each noon. For instance, the constellation Orion lies on the meridian at midnight in mid-December, but at 2 a.m. in November, and 10 p.m. in February. And, Orion isn't even visible between June and August.

There are constellations that are visible all night, every night of the year. These are what are known as the circumpolar constellations, such as the Big Dipper in the Northern Hemisphere and the Crux in the Southern Hemisphere.

Since a constellation rises two hours later each month, you can tell the time if you know when a circumpolar constellation is to lie on the meridian. To make the process simpler, build this constellation clock.

Purpose of the project:
To see how the motion of the stars throughout the year can reveal the time, just as the motion of the Sun does during the day.

What you'll need:
- White cardboard
- Paper fastener
- Rubber cement
- Tracing paper
- Patterns on these two pages

What to do:
Trace or photocopy the patterns for this project, choosing the appropriate Big Dipper or Crux for your home in either the Northern or Southern hemisphere. Glue them to cardboard and cut the patterns out. Poke holes in the center crosses, and fasten the two patterns together with a paper fastener. On the next clear night, go outside and face north (if you're in the Northern Hemisphere) or south (if you're in the Southern Hemisphere). Turn the constellation wheel so the constellation matches the stars. Find the date . . . and the correct time will be right above it!

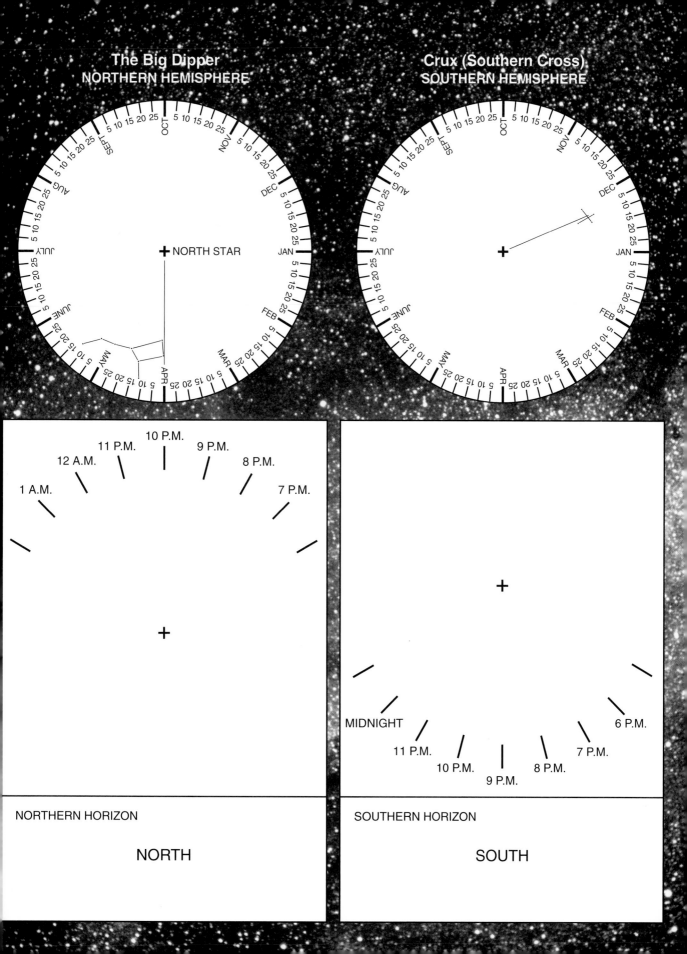

The Big Dipper
NORTHERN HEMISPHERE

Crux (Southern Cross)
SOUTHERN HEMISPHERE

+ NORTH STAR

NORTHERN HORIZON

NORTH

SOUTHERN HORIZON

SOUTH

Project 11:
True North

Knowing how to find true north may come in handy one day. And it's more accurate than using a compass.

Everyone has an idea of what north is. It's a direction the needle on a compass points, right? Well, that's not exactly true north. The needle points to Earth's magnetic pole, which is close to, but not exactly at, Earth's true North Pole.

This project will help you find true north.

Purpose of the project:
To find true north.

What you'll need:
- String
- Four long sticks
- Masking tape
- A pencil or piece of chalk

What to do:
Push a stick firmly into the ground. Tilt it until it casts a shadow (yellow dotted line). Write a *W* on a piece of tape and attach it to another stick. Push the *W* stick into the ground right at the end of the shadow from the first stick.

As the Sun moves, the shadow will move, too. After an hour or two, mark the end of the shadow with another stick with an *E* taped to it. The line between the two sticks (red dotted line) is exactly the east-west line.

But where are north and south? Make a loop on one end of a string and tie it to a fourth stick. (The string should be a bit shorter than the distance between the *W* and *E* sticks.) Tie the other end to the *E* stick. Hold the last stick so the string is tight and use it to scratch a circle in the ground. Repeat this with the loop around the *W* stick.

Stand so that the *W* stick is on your left and the *E* stick is on your right. Place the stick with the string tied to it where the circles meet closest to you. Label it with an *S*. Push your first stick into the other spot where the circles meet. That is the north stick. Wrap the loose end of the string around it. The string runs exactly north and south, pointing exactly at the true north and south ends of the Earth's axis of rotation – the North and South poles.

Project 12:
A Step Back in "Time"

Today, we rely on clocks to tell us when to leave for school and work, keep an appointment, and so on.

But people in early times did not have clocks. They knew the time of day by observing the Sun's position in the sky and by using devices called sundials. As the Sun appeared to move across the sky, the shadow on the sundial moved along the sundial's clock face.

A few hundred years ago, when people began to carry watches for the first time, you might have seen someone setting a watch according to the time on a sundial!

Stonehenge, a stone monument near Salisbury, England, is thousands of years old. Its precise alignment in relation to the rising and setting Sun has led many people to wonder whether it might have been an ancient calendar.

Purpose of the project:
To tell time from the Sun by building your own sundial.

What you'll need:
- A pencil or marker
- A 12-inch- (30-cm) long dowel
- A hammer
- A large sheet of white cardboard or paper
- A reliable watch or clock

What to do:
Find a level spot outdoors that's in direct sunlight for most or all of the day. Place your cardboard or paper on the ground. With a hammer, drive the dowel through the cardboard or paper into the ground. Make sure the dowel is standing straight and the cardboard or paper is flat.

Look on the cardboard or paper to see where the shadow of the dowel falls. Every hour on the hour during daylight, mark the cardboard or paper at the end point of the shadow. Be sure not to move the cardboard or paper as you mark it.

You now have a primitive clock. Repeat the experiment with the same piece of cardboard or paper for several days to make sure all your markings are in the right place. Then label each hourly marking (noon, 1 p.m., 2 p.m., and so forth).

Wait several months, then set up your sundial again. Have the shadows changed? What effect does daylight saving time or the changing of the seasons have on your sundial? Can you think of any places on our planet where a sundial would not work? Why not? Do you think a "moondial" or "stardial" could be an accurate timekeeper?

Project 13:
Catch a Spinning Planet

We know Earth is always spinning, but how can this be proven? With a 35mm camera, it's made very clear.

In the night sky, the stars appear to move from east to west. Of course, in reality, it is the Earth that is rotating from west to east.

A long-exposure photograph taken with a 35mm camera can capture the motion of stars on film in the form of "star trails."

If you aim your camera toward the North or South poles, your photo will reveal the star trails forming a circle around the center of rotation.

You can also take photos of constellations. Just for fun, find the stars that make up your astrological sign, and take a photo.

Below: A long exposure photograph of star trails.

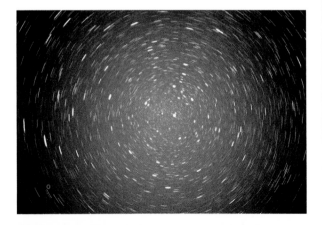

Purpose of the Project:
To show the rotation of the night sky. . . and of Earth.

What you'll need:
- A 35mm camera with a manual shutter
- A shutter cable release, available at a camera store
- Fast film – ISO 400 speed or greater
- A tripod
- A notebook

What to do:
Load the camera with film, and take a few photos of a bright, daytime scene. This will help the film lab cut the negatives properly.

On a clear, moonless night, go outside with your camera and attach the cable release according to the instructions found in your camera's manual. Set the camera's focus to infinity. Set the aperture to the smallest f/ number. Set the shutter speed to *B*.

Mount the camera on the tripod. Aim the camera at Polaris, if you're in the Northern Hemisphere, or toward Crux if you're in the Southern Hemisphere. With the cable release, open the shutter for about a minute, then close it. Advance the film, and take a few more shots. Try exposures of 5, 10, and 30 minutes. The longer the exposure time, the longer the star trails will be.

If you take pictures of other constellations, keep your shots under one minute. Experiment with times of 10, 20, 30, 45, and 60 seconds. Keep a record of all your shots, so you know which exposures produced the best results.

Your photos will show star trails tracing arcs around the celestial pole, revealing the rotation pattern of the night sky.

To attempt to create complete circles, you would have to leave the shutter open 24 hours – but daylight would ruin the shot!

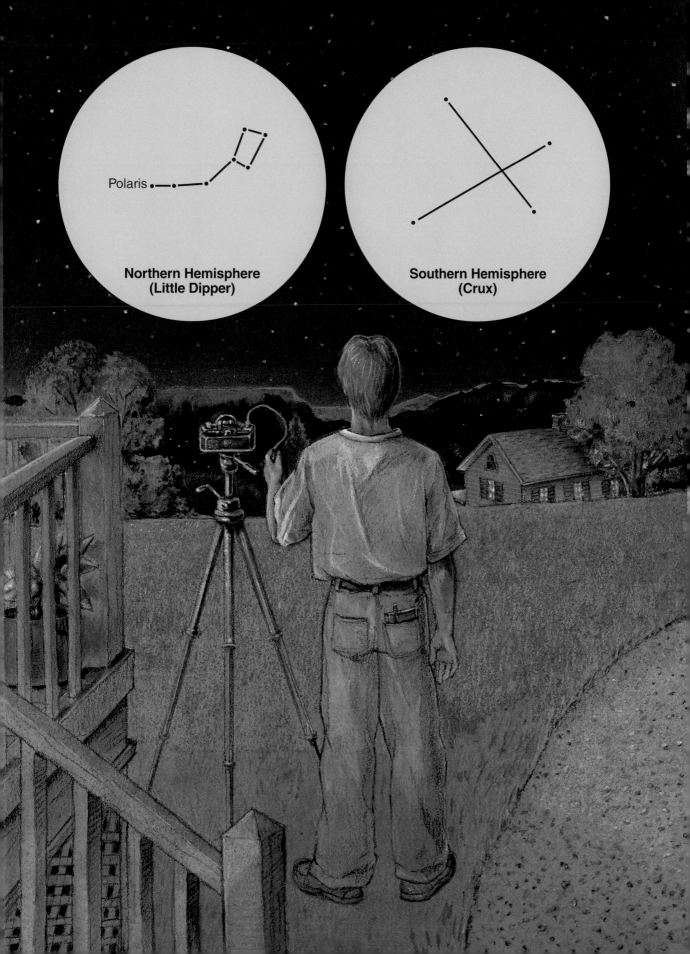

Northern Hemisphere
(Little Dipper)

Polaris

Southern Hemisphere
(Crux)

More Books Featuring Astronomy Projects

3-D Star Maps. Monkhouse and Cox (Harper & Row)

Astronomy Projects for Young Scientists. Apfel (Arco)

Far Out: How to Create Your Own Star World. West (Carolrhoda Books)

Look to the Night Sky: An Introduction to Star Watching. Simon (Penguin)

Magic Mud and Other Great Experiments. Penrose (Simon and Schuster)

Projects in Space Science. Gardner (Julian Messner)

Science Fare: An Illustrated Guide and Catalog of Toys, Books, and Activities for Kids.
    Saul and Newman (Harper & Row)

A Stargazer's Guide. Asimov (Gareth Stevens)

Whitney's Star Finder. Whitney (Knopf)

Videos

Astronomy 101: A Beginner's Guide to the Night Sky. (Mazon)

Astronomy Today. (Gareth Stevens)

Our Solar System. (Gareth Stevens)

Places to Visit

Perth Observatory
Walnut Road
Bickley, W.A. 6076 Australia

National Air and Space Museum
Smithsonian Institution
Seventh Street and Independence Avenue SW
Washington, D.C. 20560

Ontario Science Centre
770 Don Mills Road
Don Mills, Ontario M3C 1T3

International Women's Air and
    Space Museum
One Chamber Plaza
Dayton, OH 45402

Places to Contact

Here are some places you can write or contact by telephone or computer for more information about astronomy. Be sure to state what kind of information you would like.

The Planetary Society
65 North Catalina
Pasadena, CA 91106

National Museum of Science and Technology
P. O. Box 9724 – Station T
Ottawa, Ontario K1G 5A3

Sydney Observatory
P. O. Box K346
Haymarket 2000 Australia

National Space Society
922 Pennsylvania Avenue SE
Washington, D.C. 20003

For up-to-date sky watching information, call **Night Watch**
    (Adler Planetarium, Chicago, Illinois) 312-922-7827.

Online services with active astronomy areas: GEnie, America Online, and CompuServe.

Glossary

atmosphere: the gases that surround a planet, star, or moon.

channel: a groove, usually formed by running water.

constellation: a grouping of stars in the sky that seems to trace out a familiar figure or symbol. Constellations are often named after the shapes that people think they resemble.

crater: a hole or pit on a planet or moon created by volcanic explosions or the impact of meteors.

dark nebulae: vast clouds of dust and gas that do not give off much light of their own or are too far from neighboring stars to reflect much light. Dark nebulae obscure portions of the Milky Way from our view.

eclipse: the partial or complete blocking of light from one astronomical body by another one.

erosion: the process of being worn away, bit by bit, usually by wind or water.

light-year: the distance light travels in one year – nearly 6 trillion miles (9.6 trillion km).

meteor: a chunk of matter that has entered Earth's atmosphere in a fiery blaze. Also, the streak of light made as the chunk of matter enters or moves through the atmosphere.

nebula: a cloud of dust and gas in space. Some large nebulae are the birthplace of stars. Other nebulae are the debris of dying stars.

orbit: the path that one celestial object follows as it circles, or revolves, around another.

phases: the periods when an object, such as Venus, Mercury, or our Moon, is partly lit by the Sun. It takes about one month for Earth's Moon to progress through the phases of full Moon back to full Moon.

prism: a transparent object that breaks white light up into the colors of the spectrum.

refract: to bend or break up light as it passes through a prism.

"seas": the name for the flat, dark areas on the Moon, even though they are completely waterless. Any one of these "seas" is actually called a *mare*.

spectrum: the colors that appear when white light is broken up by a prism. You can see the colors of the spectrum in a rainbow.

sundial: an instrument to measure the time of day by the movement and location of the Sun.

Index

Born in 1920, Isaac Asimov came to the United States as a young boy from his native Russia. As a young man, he was a student of biochemistry. In time, he became one of the most productive writers the world has ever known. His books cover a spectrum of topics, including science, history, language theory, fantasy, and science fiction. His brilliant imagination gained him the respect and admiration of adults and children alike. Sadly, Isaac Asimov died shortly after the publication of the first edition of *Isaac Asimov's Library of the Universe*.

The publishers wish to thank the following for permission to reproduce copyright material: front cover, 5 (large), 7, 9, 10-11, 15 (large), 17, 19, 21 (large), 25, 27, 29 (large), Tom Redman; 5 (insets), Matthew Groshek/© Gareth Stevens, Inc.; 6, Jet Propulsion Laboratory; 8, © George East; 12, © Jon Allyn M. Photog., Cr.; 13, © Gareth Stevens, Inc. 1995; 14, © James R. Peterson 1986; 15 (inset), Matthew Groshek/© Gareth Stevens, Inc.; 16, © Dennis Milon 1980; 19 (insets), 20, 21 (insets), Matthew Groshek/© Gareth Stevens, Inc.; 22, 23 (insets), © Gareth Stevens, Inc. 1995; 22-23, © Fred Espenak; 28, Greg Walz-Chojnacki; 29 (insets), © Gareth Stevens, Inc. 1995.